BASEBALL TREASURES

By STEPHEN WONG

photographs by SUSAN EINSTEIN

 Smithsonian | Collins

An Imprint of HarperCollinsPublishers

SMITHSONIAN MISSION STATEMENT

For more than 160 years, the Smithsonian has remained true to its mission, "the increase and diffusion of knowledge." Today the Smithsonian is not only the world's largest provider of museum experiences supported by authoritative scholarship in science, history, and the arts but also an international leader in scientific research and exploration. The Smithsonian offers the world a picture of America, and America a picture of the world.

The Corey R. Shanus Collection: iv, 1, 2; The Dr. Mark W. Cooper Collection: 8; The Greg Gallacher Collection: front jacket, 2, 3, 4, 11, 12, 13, 14, 17, 18; The Brian Seigel Collection: front jacket, i, 32, 33, 34; The Dr. Richard C. Angrist Collection: front and back jacket, v, 5, 6, 8, 10, 19, 20, 28, 29; The Nick Depace Family Collection: front jacket, 22, 23, 24, 25, 26, 27, 29; The Marshall Fogel Collection: back jacket, v, 8, 31, 32, 38–39, 40–41, 52, 56; The James and Lauren Clister Collection: back jacket, iii, 38, 39, 40, 41, 42, 43; The Robert Edward Lifson Collection: back jacket, iv, 38; The Penny Marshall Collection: back jacket, 3, 7; The Charles M. Merkel Collection: front jacket, i, v, 30, 34, 35, 36, 37, 38; The Ron Leff Family Collection: 20, 45, 46, 47, 48, 49; The Bill Mastro Collection: front and back jacket, v, 5, 37, 56; The David Bowen Collection: front jacket; The Todd McFarlane Collection: 9; The Wong Family Archives Collection: front jacket, iv, vi, 1, 15, 21, 23, 28, 38, 39, 44, 50, 51, 52, 53, 54, 55, 56, 57; © John Zich/Newsport/CORBIS: 6; © Duomo/CORBIS: 7; Courtesy of the Louisville Slugger Museum: 20; © Bettmann/CORBIS: 24, 25, 26, 38, 45, 47, 49, 57; © AP/World Wide Photos: 27; © Topps Company, Inc.: back jacket, 30, 31, 32, 52

The name of the Smithsonian, Smithsonian Institution and the sunburst logo are registered trademarks of the Smithsonian Institution.
Collins is an imprint of HarperCollins Publishers.

Library of Congress Cataloging-in-Publication Data
Wong, Stephen.
　Baseball treasures / by Stephen Wong ; photographs by Susan Einstein. — 1st ed.
　　p.　cm.
　ISBN-10: 0-06-114464-9 (trade bdg.) — ISBN-13: 978-0-06-114464-6 (trade bdg.)
　ISBN-10: 0-06-114473-8 (lib. bdg.) — ISBN-13: 978-0-06-114473-8 (lib. bdg.)
　1. Baseball—Collectibles—United States—Juvenile literature.　2. Baseball—History—Juvenile literature.　I. Einstein, Susan.　II. Title.
GV875.2.W65　2007　　　　　　　　　　　　　　　　　　　　　2006036069
796.3570973'075—dc22

Design by Charles Yuen
1 2 3 4 5 6 7 8 9 10
❖
First Edition

For my sister Adrianna, Uncle Bill, Aunty Michelle, Uncle Samson, Aunty Joan, and our dear family friend, Judy Sin
—S.W.

CONTENTS

Souvenir of WORLD SERIES RED SOX vs. ST. LOUIS CARDINALS Boston, Mass. 1946

Pennant sold at Fenway Park
during the 1946 World Series

1941 pin-back of Lou Gehrig

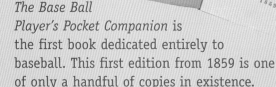

*The Base Ball
Player's Pocket Companion* is
the first book dedicated entirely to
baseball. This first edition from 1859 is one
of only a handful of copies in existence.

When I was in high school, I read a famous book about baseball called *The Glory of Their Times: The Story of the Early Days of Baseball Told by the Men Who Played It*. In the book, old-time greats talk about playing in the major leagues during the heyday of Hall of Famers such as Babe Ruth, Ty Cobb, and Lou Gehrig. The book is full of colorful characters and their amazing stories. I was already a huge baseball fan and collector of baseball cards. *The Glory of Their Times* deepened my love of the game and my understanding of it.

I learned all I could about the history of the sport. I also began expanding my collection of baseball memorabilia. On top of baseball cards, I started collecting old scorecards, black-and-white photographs, World Series ticket stubs, and eventually bats and uniforms once worn by players. Collecting became my passion. Everything in my collection pays tribute to the glories of baseball's rich heritage.

More than twenty years after first reading *The Glory of Their Times*, I had the idea to write a book of my own. As a collector of baseball memorabilia, I thought it would be interesting to write about the world's finest private collections of baseball artifacts. I wanted to hear the stories of other passionate collectors—how they got started, what made them do it, what teams and players and objects they loved best. Plus, it would be really exciting to see the rare and priceless things they owned. Bats once swung by Babe Ruth! A jersey worn by Hammerin' Hank Aaron! Real World Series championship trophies!

All those objects and many more are featured in *Baseball Treasures*. In addition to highlighting special collections and the different types of artifacts they contain, this book traces the history of collecting—and through it, the history of the game itself. The objects bring readers closer to timeless players such as Ruth, Cobb, Gehrig, Robinson, Wagner, and so many others, capturing the glory of the national pastime through their feats on and off the field.

While writing the book, I realized that my journey was about more than the outstanding collections I'd seen. It was really about the very soul of baseball. As author Tom Stanton wrote: "Baseball's appeal isn't complicated or confusing. It's about the beauty of a game; it's about heroes and family and friends; it's about being part of something larger than yourself, about belonging; it's about tradition—receiving it and passing it on; and it's about holding on to a bit of your childhood."

That is how we baseball collectors feel. And this book is my way of sharing those feelings with young fans. Just as I was inspired by *The Glory of Their Times* all those years ago, I hope *Baseball Treasures* inspires a passion for the game and its colorful history in a whole new generation of readers.

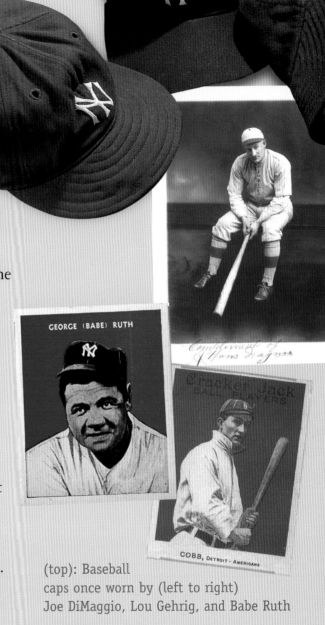

(top): Baseball caps once worn by (left to right) Joe DiMaggio, Lou Gehrig, and Babe Ruth

(middle): 1912 autographed studio portrait of Honus Wagner; 1932 United States Caramel baseball card of Babe Ruth; 1915 Cracker Jack baseball card of Ty Cobb

(left): Official National League baseball autographed by each member of the 1955 World Champion Brooklyn Dodgers

Lou Gehrig's game-worn jersey and cap, game-used bat, and pennant from the New York Yankees' 1937 American League title, and a 1939 World Series program with Lou Gehrig on the cover

1

BALLS

YOU CAN'T PLAY BASEBALL without a ball. Maybe that's why so many fans of the game love to collect them. A game-used baseball reminds us of great players and amazing plays. You can hold a ball in your hand and see Sandy Koufax kicking high and throwing a strike-three heater right past a batter. You can imagine Mickey Mantle cranking it into the upper deck for a game-winning homer. The red-stitched baseball is the heart of the game.

(above): Actual baseball used in the 1911 Addie Joss Day Benefit Game and a T205 baseball card of Addie Joss from 1911 issued by the American Tobacco Company

(right): The earliest known trophy ball in existence was used in the New York Knickerbocker Club and the Gotham Club of New York match on July 5, 1853. It was made into a trophy commemorating the fiftieth anniversary of the game.

[1]

Some fans collect baseballs signed by their favorite players or teams. Others collect balls to celebrate monumental events, like the actual ball thrown by a pitcher in a no-hitter.

A collector named Gregory John Gallacher likes a different type of ball. Mr. Gallacher collects really old baseballs. Some of the balls in his collection go back to the very earliest days of baseball, about 150 years ago, when the sport was just beginning to catch on with American boys.

Some of Mr. Gallacher's baseballs don't even look like baseballs. They're smaller than the ones we use today and have different kinds of stitching. Some of the very oldest ones are homemade. Players who wanted to start up a game sometimes made their own balls. Homemade baseballs were often pretty soft. They had to be. Back then it was legal to drill a runner with a ball to get him out!

America's first professional baseball league was called the National Association of Base Ball Players. In 1861, the league decided that all official baseballs should be roughly the same size and weight. Before that, the size, weight, and material of each ball were rarely similar. What the ball looked like depended on who made it and what kind of materials he could get. One popular way to construct balls in the 1830s and 1840s

(above left): Collector Greg Gallacher in a nineteenth-century baseball uniform with a ring bat from the 1880s

(above): Actual game-used baseball from an October 21, 1861 baseball game played at Elysian Fields in Hoboken, New Jersey

(right): Handmade folk art display of baseballs signed by all 1942 American League team members

(below): Early-twentieth-century viselike device for holding a ball in place while it is stitched

NEW YORK
.669

BOSTON
.612

ST. LOUIS
.543

CLEVELAND
.487

AMERICAN
1942
LEAGUE

DETROIT
.474

CHICAGO
.446

WASHINGTON
.411

PHILADELPHIA
.357

was to make a core of rubber strips and string, and then cover it with four strips of leather. This early type of ball is known as the lemon-peel ball, because the leather strips look like lemon wedges. Lemon-peel balls were popular until around 1870.

Another kind of ball was the "belt ball." The cover of the belt ball was made from a single strip of leather. The leather was cut and stitched to form a sphere. The stitching on a belt ball formed the pattern of a letter *H* on one side of the ball. The other side had no seams at all.

By the 1870s, ball makers started using two panels of cowhide as covers. They stitched the covers together in a figure-eight pattern. Rawlings, the company that makes official major-league baseballs, uses the same pattern today.

Baseball collector Dr. Richard C. Angrist has an amazing collection of autographed balls. Many celebrate the great teams of his youth. When Dr. Angrist was a boy growing up in New York, the city had three pro baseball teams. He and his dad rooted for the Brooklyn Dodgers. The other teams were the New York Yankees and the New York Giants. In the 1940s and 1950s, the New York teams were the best in the game. At least one of them made it to the World Series for ten straight years.

(left): An 1850s handmade lemon-peel baseball

(middle): An 1870s belt ball made from one strip of leather

(bottom): An 1870s pigskin ball features the modern-day figure-eight stitching pattern

But the Yankees were a little bit better than even the Dodgers or the Giants. From the 1940s through the early 1950s, the Dodgers lost five times to the Yankees in the World Series.

The tide turned in 1955. That year, the Dodgers finally toppled the Yankees. They beat them four games to three in one of the greatest World Series ever played. Today, Dr. Angrist owns a ball signed by all the 1955 Dodgers. It is the showpiece of his fabulous collection of autographed baseballs.

Not every vintage ball in Dr. Angrist's collection pays tribute to the Dodgers. Some were signed by their archrivals, the Yankees. Two of the greatest teams in history were the 1927 and 1932 Yankees. The Yanks won the World Series both years. Dr. Angrist owns Yankees team-signed balls from both of these World Series teams. These were the record-setting teams of legends Lou Gehrig and Babe Ruth.

You could say that Ruth revolutionized the home run. Before the Bambino started blasting shots out of ballparks, the round-tripper wasn't a big part of the game. Ruth's mammoth blasts single-handedly won games. Fans loved his power.

Many years later, modern fans fell in love with three new home-run kings. Mark McGwire, Sammy Sosa, and Barry Bonds belted more

(above): New York Yankees team-signed baseballs from 1927 (left) and 1932 (right)

(below): Original 1927 photograph from a postseason barnstorming tour that featured Babe Ruth and Lou Gehrig

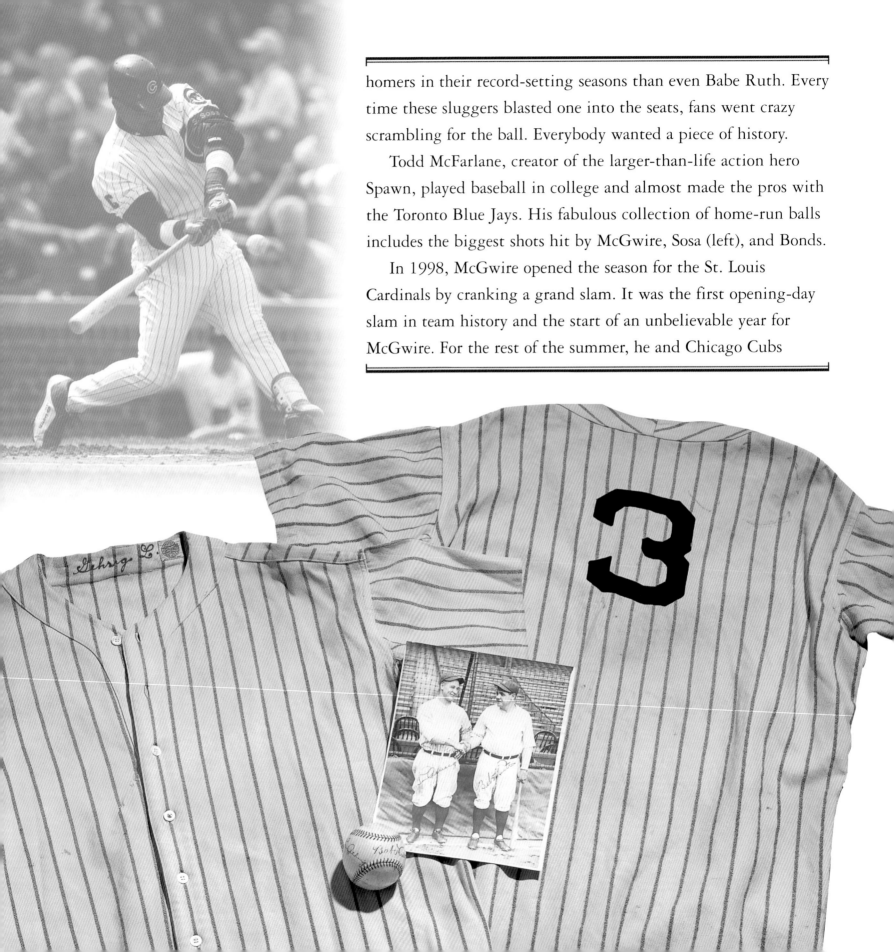

homers in their record-setting seasons than even Babe Ruth. Every time these sluggers blasted one into the seats, fans went crazy scrambling for the ball. Everybody wanted a piece of history.

Todd McFarlane, creator of the larger-than-life action hero Spawn, played baseball in college and almost made the pros with the Toronto Blue Jays. His fabulous collection of home-run balls includes the biggest shots hit by McGwire, Sosa (left), and Bonds.

In 1998, McGwire opened the season for the St. Louis Cardinals by cranking a grand slam. It was the first opening-day slam in team history and the start of an unbelievable year for McGwire. For the rest of the summer, he and Chicago Cubs outfielder Sammy Sosa battled each other to see who could break the record for home runs in a season. The record belonged to Roger Maris, who hit 61 homers in 1961. That was one more than the Babe had hit in 1927.

All season long, Sosa and McGwire (right) sent balls flying out of parks around the National League. Every time either guy came up to bat, there was a chance he'd knock one out. In the month of June alone, Sosa homered 20 times—the most ever hit by a major leaguer in a single month. He was chasing history, but he couldn't catch McGwire. On September 8, Big Mac slugged number 62 to break Maris's time-honored mark. The burly redhead finished the season with a staggering 70 home runs. Sosa ended up with 66. Throughout the race, the two players showed a lot of respect for each other.

"It doesn't matter if [McGwire] plays for the Cardinals and I play for Chicago," Sosa said after one Cubs-Cardinals game. "We still have a relationship as people, as friends." Fans loved that kind of sportsmanship.

Mr. McFarlane's collection from that historic year includes McGwire's 1st and 70th home-run balls as well as Sosa's 66th. A few years later he added another trophy to his collection: home run 73 hit by Barry Bonds in 2001. The

(left): 1940s Official League baseball radio

(facing page, bottom): 1932 game-worn home jerseys of Lou Gehrig and Babe Ruth, along with an autographed photograph and baseball signed by both players

seemingly impossible numbers put up by Sosa and McGwire lasted for only three seasons before Bonds beat everybody. News about steroid use in major-league baseball has raised questions about the 1998 season, and later ones, but at the time the race to pass 61 and 70 homers captured the imagination of every baseball fan.

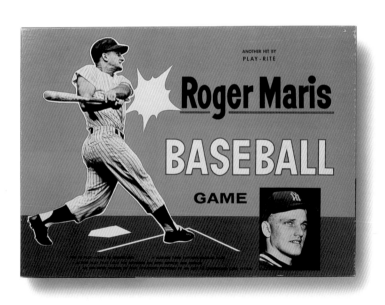

(above): Play-Rite's Roger Maris Baseball Game came out in 1962, the year after Maris broke the single-season home-run record of 60.

(top right): Circa 1927 die-cut advertising display for *The Sporting News,* featuring Babe Ruth

(right): Roger Maris in 1961

(facing page): Mark McGwire's record-setting 70th home-run ball; Barry Bonds's record-setting 73rd home-run ball; Sammy Sosa's 66th home-run ball

TRADE MARK
George "Babe" Ruth
REG. U.S. PAT. OFF.
HILLERICH & BRADSBY CO.
MADE IN U.S.A.
LOUISVILLE, KY.
TRADE MARK
George "Babe" Ruth
REG. U.S. PAT. OFF.
LOUISVILLE SLUGGER
125
HILLERICH & BRADSBY CO.
MADE IN U.S.A.
TRADE MARK
George "Babe" Ruth
REG. U.S. PAT. OFF.
LOUISVILLE SLUGGER
125
HILLERICH & BRADSBY CO.
MADE IN U.S.A.
LOUISVILLE, KY.
TRADE MARK
George "Babe" Ruth
"Babe" Ruth
TRADE MARK
George "Babe" Ruth
REG. U.S. PAT. OFF.
HILLERICH & BRADSBY CO.
MADE IN U.S.A.
TRADE MARK
George "Babe" Ruth
REG. U.S. PAT. OFF.
LOUISVILLE SLUGGER
125
HILLERICH & BRADSBY CO.
TRADE MARK

CHAPTER

2

GLOVES AND BATS

IMAGINE HOW EXCITING IT WOULD BE to swing a bat that Babe Ruth once used to hit a home run. You would be gripping history in your hands!

Dr. Richard C. Angrist owns just such a bat. In fact, Dr. Angrist owns eight different bats that belonged to the Bambino. One bat even has notches that the Babe carved into it to keep track of his homers.

(facing page): Eight game-used Babe Ruth Louisville Sluggers that the Bambino used during his legendary career

(right): A Rawlings fielder's glove from the 1980s

Dr. Angrist collects only baseball items that were used by real players in actual games. Other fans collect the oldest gloves and bats they can find. Rather than looking for stuff used by famous players, they try to find equipment dating from the earliest days of baseball.

Gregory John Gallacher has a world-class collection of antique baseball gloves and bats. Some of the gear in his collection is more than 150 years old. It goes all the way back to the Civil War era, when baseball started to spread across the country.

The crescent-heel glove, from the 1890s, takes its name from the heavy padding at its base.

GLOVES

Old gloves don't look anything like what today's players use. They're small and have hardly any padding. Catching a ball with one would hurt!

When baseball started, fielders didn't wear gloves at all. Things began to change around 1875. That's when Charles C. Waitt, a first baseman for the St. Louis Brown Stockings, started wearing a small, tight glove in games. His glove was made of leather. It was called a fingerless glove, because it covered only the palm of his hand.

A couple of years later, Chicago White Stockings first baseman Albert Goodwill Spalding also started to wear a fingerless glove. In addition to playing baseball, Spalding ran a sporting goods business. He thought if he wore a glove in games, the idea would catch on. Then his sporting goods business would sell more gloves. He was right. Within a few years, fielders at every position were wearing gloves like Spalding's.

A first baseman's mitt from 1900 also features crescent-shaped padding.

A fielder's glove from the 1890s features a ribbed, spiral pattern to help secure the ball in the pocket.

Derived from the Bill Doak model, a fielder's glove from the 1930s features leather lacing between the fingers.

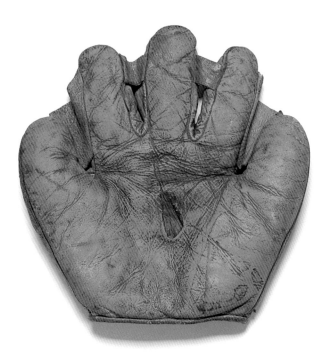

An "ambidextrous" glove from 1900

A "pita pocket" glove made of white buckskin from 1900

Around 1882, Worcester Ruby Legs third baseman Arthur Irwin became the first player to use padding in his glove. He had hurt his hand, and he wore the glove to protect it. His glove had fingers and was like a small leather pillow that fit over his hand. It was called a workman's glove. This style of glove soon became popular with other players.

Soon gloves began to change in shape and design. New models had more padding in the palm or stitching to help players grip the ball. Crescent-heel gloves had a big wedge of padding in the heel to help fielders cradle the ball.

In the 1920s, Bill Doak, a spitball pitcher for the St. Louis Cardinals, created the first truly modern glove. The Doak model was much smaller than today's mitts, but it did have padding, a pocket area, and leather laces between the fingers. Playing defense got a lot easier.

(above right): A three-fingered glove from the 1920s

(right): Original photograph from the 1880s of a Long Island ballplayer with a fingerless glove on his left hand for throwing and a workman's glove on his right. A fingerless glove from the 1880s has been added to the upper right corner of the photo.

BATS

Bats have been around even longer than the game of baseball. Hundreds of years before baseball was played in the United States, children in England played batting games called trap-ball and rounders.

Early baseball bats were modeled after rounders bats. Many of Mr. Gallacher's old-time bats have huge knobs on the bottom of the handles. Others have flat sides. One bat in Mr. Gallacher's collection is called a Massachusetts-style bat. It is named after the Massachusetts game, an early form of baseball based on rounders.

In the 1880s, bat makers tried out lots of different designs. Mr. Gallacher's collection includes many models that look strange today. Flat bats, which were flattened along the barrel, were supposed to make it easier for batters to hit the ball accurately.

Another early type of bat was the spring-handled bat. This has a skinny handle and a fat hitting surface. In theory, spring-handled bats were supposed to act like whips and give a batter extra power. These didn't last long, either, because power hitting was not a big part of the sport in baseball's early days. Contact hitting and hit-and-run plays made up the preferred style of play called the scientific game.

(below): Game-used bats, including Rogers Hornsby's bat (middle) from his National League Most Valuable Player 1929 season, along with bats of (from left to right) Charlie Grimm, Hack Wilson, Kiki Cuyler, and Riggs Stephenson

Lots of early bats were designed to help batters at the scientific game. The Spalding "mushroom" bat from 1906 has a large knob on the handle. The knob balanced the weight of the bat, making it easier for hitters to control their swings. Other odd bats of this era included the Lajoie double-handled bat. Instead of one knob at the handle end, it has two. It was named for legendary Cleveland Naps second baseman Napoleon Lajoie.

Game-used bat collectors like Dr. Angrist look for three things to help them know if a bat was used by a player. First, they study a bat to see if it is marked in any special way. Players sometimes taped or scratched the handles of their bats to make them easier to grip. For example, Hall of Fame first baseman Hank Greenberg always scratched up his bat handle with a bottle cap.

Second, collectors try to find bats that are autographed by players. If a player autographed a bat, he must have at least held it in his hands.

Third, collectors study the records kept by Hillerich & Bradsby Company. H & B, as the company is called, has been making the famous Louisville Slugger baseball bats for more than one hundred years. It has kept track of virtually every single professional model bat it has shipped since 1930, and some of its records date as far back as the early twentieth century.

Years ago when a player needed a new bat, he would send his old one back to the H & B factory in Kentucky. Workers wrote in grease pencil the player's name and team on the side, and noted the bat's size and weight and the date the player sent it back. They used the old bat as a model to make a new one.

The notes on the side of a bat are called "side-writing." Today, collectors like Dr. Angrist use side-writing to find out who actually used the bat. For example, Hall of Fame Yankee Joe

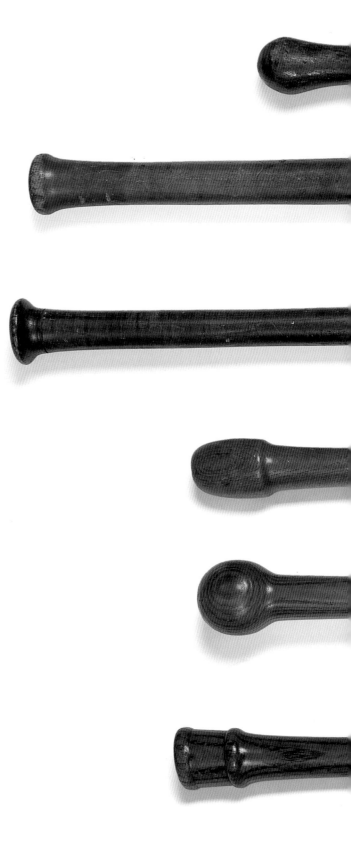

A circa-1840s "Massachusetts-style" bat made from an axe handle

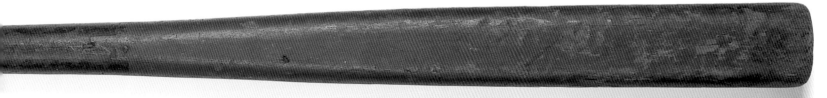

A circa-1885 "flat bat," designed to aid hit-and-run batting techniques, like bunting

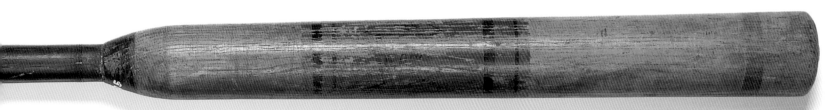

The short-lived "spring-handled" bat appeared at the dawn of the twentieth century.

Greg Gallacher's Spalding "mushroom" bat dates to around 1906 and was designed to give hitters a more even distribution of weight.

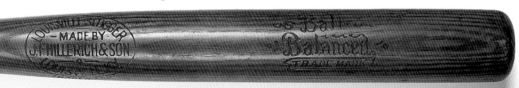

J. F. Hillerich & Son, maker of the famous Louisville Slugger, issued this "ball-balanced" bat—clearly influenced by the mushroom bat—circa 1908.

Named for Hall of Fame second baseman Nap Lajoie, Gallacher's Wright & Ditson double-handled bat dates to about 1910.

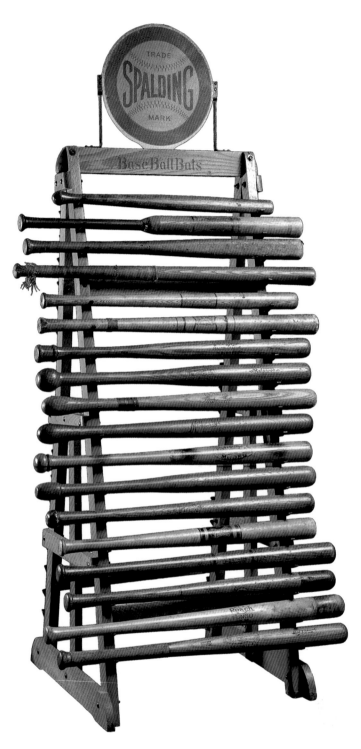

A Spalding bat rack was a common feature in early-twentieth-century sporting goods stores.

DiMaggio used a Joe DiMaggio signature-model bat. Joltin' Joe was one of the best hitters who ever lived, so naturally many of his teammates used Joe DiMaggio professional signature-model bats, too. If a Joe DiMaggio model bat was returned to the factory by one of his teammates, then the teammate's name would be written on the side—not DiMaggio's.

Hillerich & Bradsby also kept track of bats by burning letters and numbers into their knobs. These codes are called vault marks. The company assigned different vault marks to different players. When powerful hitter Jimmie Foxx sent back one bat to have an exact copy made, H & B marked it F3. The F stood for Foxx. The 3 meant this bat was the third style made for him. Foxx sent back an F3 model bat for a new one in 1931. The next two years, he led the major leagues in home runs, outslugging even Babe Ruth. It must have been a good bat!

Dr. Angrist's amazing collection includes many side-written, vault-marked, and autographed bats. He owns bats that once belonged to almost every record-setting hitter ever to play the game. It is one of baseball's most famous and valuable collections.

THE WAZIR OF WHAM

Baseball fans had never seen anyone like Babe Ruth. When the Babe clouted a record 29 round-trippers in 1919, people jumped for joy. The Babe was larger than life, a true national hero. A year later, he crushed an astounding 54 homers. In the whole American League, no other team hit that many. Ruth was even better in 1921. That year, he smashed 59 dingers. A few seasons later, in 1927, he outdid himself one more time, hitting an even 60.

With each blast, Ruth's legend grew. Sportswriters tried to come up with bigger, bolder nicknames for the slugger. They called him the Bambino, the Sultan of Swat, the Maharajah of Mash, and the Wazir of Wham. By the time he retired in 1935, he held 56 major-league batting records. In fact, he set a record number of records.

No wonder collectors love his bats.

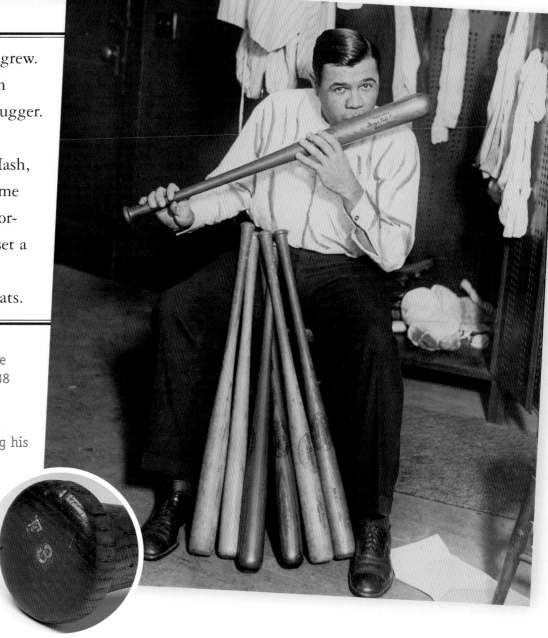

(above): Grease pencil side-writing on the barrel of Joe DiMaggio's bat from the 1938 season

(right): Original news service photo from September 29, 1926, of Babe Ruth kissing his bats before the start of the World Series

(below right): Vault mark "F3" on the bat knob of Hall of Fame slugger Jimmie Foxx's bat

COLLECTING GAME-USED BASEBALL BATS

Bats used by professional ballplayers are different from others. Pro-model bats are made specially for players. You can't buy them in stores. Bats sold in sporting goods shops are called store-model bats. Some store-model bats are endorsed by pro stars, but the players never use them.

Hillerich & Bradsby Company makes more bats than anyone. For almost a hundred years, H & B has put a code on each of its store-model bats. The code is usually above the company's name on the barrel of a bat. The code is a number and a letter. The number is the length of the bat in inches. The letter is the initial of the player whose name is stamped on the bat. H & B also stamps the length of a store-model bat on the knob.

Collectors use these codes to tell the difference between store-model and pro-model bats. Most collectors would rather have game-used pro-model bats. Store-model bats can be very cool, but a ballplayer's game-used bat is history.

(above, top to bottom): A Napoleon Lajoie game-used bat from 1903 and 1904—the only bat from Lajoie's playing days known to exist; side-writing and a "J13" vault mark on the knob confirms this bat to be Shoeless Joe Jackson's bat from the early seasons of his career, including 1911; a specially made Mickey Mantle 1955 World Series bat

(above, right) Professional bat-order records were kept in ledgers containing handwritten dates, names, and photos.

MARKS ON GENUINE GAME-USED PRO BATS

MANUFACTURER MARKINGS

1. **CENTER BRANDS:** Since 1917, the professional model number 125 appears on just about every H & B pro bat (top).

2. **LABELS:** Genuine H & B pro-model bats have deep, burned-in labels (above and bottom).

3. **MODEL NUMBERS:** For more than sixty years, all H & B pro bats have had model numbers stamped into the knobs. The model numbers are a letter followed by one to three numbers, such as M110.

4. **SPECIAL BATS:** H & B makes special bats for the All-Star Game and the World Series. The player's name, the date, and the event are printed on each bat (facing page, bottom; this page, top).

SIGNS OF GAME USE

1. **BALL AND STITCH MARKS:** When a baseball hits a bat, it leaves a mark. Sometimes the mark is a light smudge. Sometimes it is a deeper imprint made by the stitches of the ball.

2. **RACK MARKS:** Pro baseball teams keep their bats in racks. When a player pulls out a bat to hit, it rubs against the rack. This can leave long scrapemarks on the bat.

3. **OTHER MARKINGS:** In the old days, players toughened their bats by rubbing them with hard objects, like bone or stone. Sometimes they repaired cracks by filling them with small nails.

4. **PERSONAL HABITS:** Players treat bats differently. Ty Cobb liked only black or white tape on the handle (below). Ted Williams sometimes painted his uniform number, 9, on the knob.

CHAPTER

3

JERSEYS

DO YOU REMEMBER THE FIRST BALL GAME you ever went to? Dr. Nick Depace sure does. The New Jersey–based collector was eight years old when his dad took him to Yankee Stadium more than forty years ago. From his seat, young Nick watched in awe as the first Yankee came out of the dugout to take batting practice. The player's cap hid his face, but the big number 7 on the back of his pinstriped uniform gave him away. Nick

(facing page): Lou Gehrig's home jersey from 1927 in an original 1920s locker from Yankee Stadium

(above): Robert Lewis "Hack" Wilson's home jersey from the 1930 season when he batted .356, hit 56 home runs, and drove in a major-league record 191 RBIs

(right): Mickey Mantle and Hank Aaron during the 1957 World Series

Ty Cobb's game-worn Philadelphia A's jersey from the 1927 and 1928 seasons and game-used bat from the 1920s

(inset): Ty Cobb was nicknamed "the Georgia Peach."

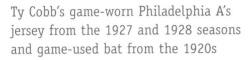

could hardly believe it. The player was none other than his hero Mickey Mantle, the great Yankees center fielder.

"I often reminisce about that day I saw Mickey Mantle for the first time in my life," Dr. Depace says. To hold on to the memories of his baseball-loving boyhood, Dr. Depace collects major-league uniforms and jerseys worn by Hall of Fame players during their stellar careers.

For a ballplayer, nothing is more special or personal than his uniform. A number 7 New York Yankees jersey, for example, means one thing and one thing only: Mickey Mantle. The Mick played for the Yankees for 18 seasons, hit 536 home runs, and helped the Yanks win 7 World Series. After Mantle hung up his spikes in 1968, the Yankees retired his number for good. No Yankee player will ever again wear number 7.

In the 1960s, some teams began placing players' names in large letters above the numbers on the backs of their jerseys. Game-worn jerseys have other marks on them, such as the team logo, name, or home city. The ballplayer's name is often stitched into the collar, the left-front tail, or the back tail of the jersey.

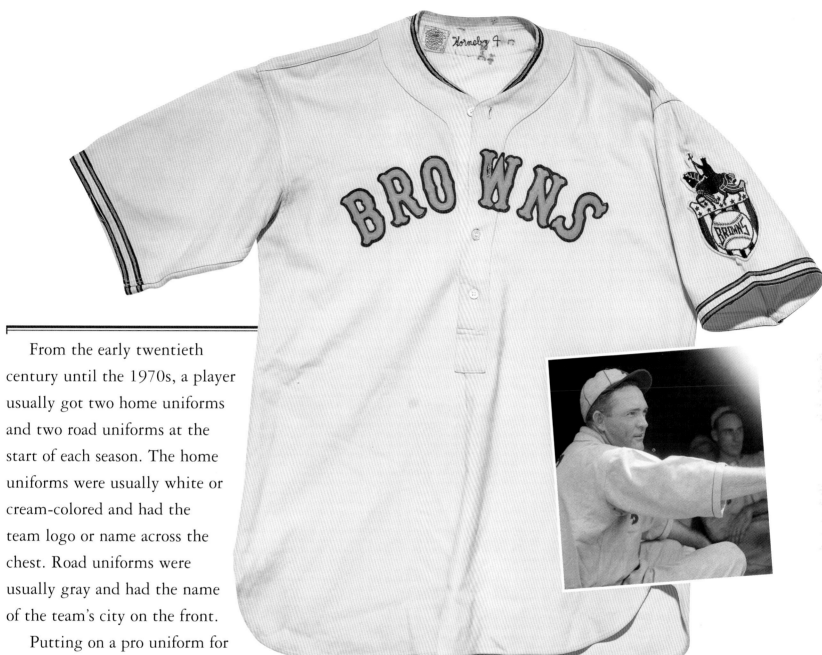

From the early twentieth century until the 1970s, a player usually got two home uniforms and two road uniforms at the start of each season. The home uniforms were usually white or cream-colored and had the team logo or name across the chest. Road uniforms were usually gray and had the name of the team's city on the front.

Putting on a pro uniform for the first time is a proud moment for any young player. Stan Hack, a beloved Chicago Cubs third baseman in the 1930s and 1940s, always remembered that milestone. "My first day with the team was unforgettable. Not because of my performance, but because I got to put on that uniform," he once said. "After the game, even though it was sweaty and soiled, I felt obliged to hang it up with the same care as I found it. As I left the locker room that day, I turned to look

A Rogers Hornsby St. Louis Browns game-worn jersey from 1937, his last season in the majors

(inset): Rogers Hornsby won the Triple Crown twice in his career for leading his league in batting average, home runs, and RBIs.

at it once more, feeling as if I was leaving a bit of myself there."

Today baseball uniform collectors prize vintage flannel uniforms from the 1940s and earlier. Back then, uniforms were made of wool or a blend of wool and cotton. They got wrinkled easily, itched, and were hot, but they looked great. Now they have the classic appeal of old-time baseball.

Dr. Depace's stunning collection captures the spirit of a bygone era. Some of the uniforms are slightly stained or soiled. Small tears or holes spark his imagination: How did they get there? Ty Cobb might have gotten his uniform dirty sliding into second base way back in 1928. The stain on the back of Jackie Robinson's jersey might be dirt from Ebbets Field, mixed with blood from a scrape Jackie got while stealing home.

Another top-shelf uniform collection belongs to Dr. Richard C. Angrist. He owns caps, jerseys, and pants worn in games by many of the all-time greats. He has the home Yankees shirt Babe Ruth wore in the 1932 World Series against the Chicago Cubs.

Boston Red Sox legend Jimmie Foxx's 1942 game-worn jersey. The Health patch on the left sleeve was to remind Americans to stay healthy to support the war effort.

(left): Jimmie Foxx won the Triple Crown in 1933.

Dr. Angrist also has home jerseys and caps worn in games by Yankees legends Lou Gehrig, Joe DiMaggio, Mickey Mantle, and Reggie Jackson. There is a special place in his collection for the Brooklyn Dodgers, the team he loved as a boy. He has the game-worn home jerseys of Dodgers heroes Jackie Robinson, Duke Snider, and Pee Wee Reese.

The uniforms owned by Dr. Angrist and Dr. Depace are more than just collections of shirts and trousers and caps. Each item is a real link to the heroes of the past.

(above): A 1949 game-worn Jackie Robinson jersey, along with the bat he used in that season's All-Star game

(left): Robinson stole home 19 times in his career.

COLLECTING GAME-WORN UNIFORMS (1900–1960s)

Game-worn uniforms, which include jerseys and pants, bring collectors closer to major-league players than just about any other item. Nothing is more personal, and no other type of baseball equipment is so scarce. In most cases, only one or two uniforms for any player are known to exist.

To find out if a vintage uniform is the real thing, collectors study a number of clues. These include the type of fabric the uniform is made of, player names on jerseys, and any obvious changes that have been made to the uniform.

FABRICS AND STYLES

Heavy wool flannel was the fabric of choice until the 1940s, when lighter wool blends came into use. During the 1960s, baseball teams converted to man-made polyester fabrics for their uniforms. These led the way to the stretchy double-knit uniforms of the 1970s and later.

PLAYERS' NAMES ON JERSEYS

From 1900 to 1920, a player's name was often stitched onto his jersey with black thread. The name was usually stitched in one of two places—the collar or the left-front tail. During the 1920s and early 1930s, some teams stitched the player's name and the year the jersey was worn on the jersey's back-right tail. From the 1930s to the 1960s, the stitching was usually done with red thread. Over the years, the color of the thread faded from red to pink.

By the mid-1930s, every major league baseball team put uniform numbers on the backs of jerseys. Even so, they continued to stitch players' names into the jerseys. In the 1940s and 1950s, many teams stitched the name—and sometimes the year or player number—on a white or gray tag that was sewn onto the collar or the left-front tail of the uniform.

ALTERATIONS

The most valuable kind of jersey is one that looks just the way it did when it came off the back of a big league player. Any change, such as the removal of the team name or logo, makes it worth less. By holding a jersey inside out against a bright light, collectors can usually see whether a player's name or number has been removed from a jersey. Darkened areas in the form

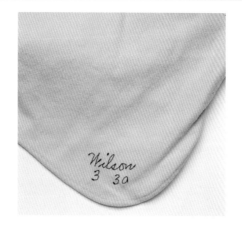

(facing page): Yogi Berra's 1953 game-worn cap and an original Milwaukee Braves road jersey that Hank Aaron wore during the 1956 and 1957 seasons. Aaron won the MVP in 1957 when the Braves added the "laughing Brave" patch to the left sleeve.

(above, from left to right): Strip tag identifies this Joe DiMaggio road jersey from the 1950 season; the "3" signifies this Hack Wilson jersey as the third of four sets from the 1930 season; Jim "Catfish" Hunter's 1968 jersey

(left): Cal Ripken's circa-1980s jersey; a jersey where the uniform number has clearly been changed

of other numbers, as well as stitching holes, show that a uniform has been altered.

If a uniform number was changed by a team during the season in which it was worn, the change may not affect the jersey's value. For example, in 1939 St. Louis outfielder Pepper Martin had his number changed from 1 to 11. This kind of "team change" is not really an alteration. It's just part of the history of the uniform during the time Martin wore it.

There is one kind of change that actually makes a jersey more valuable. This is the addition of special patches. For example, the Health patch (left) was added to the left sleeve of every jersey in the majors from 1942 to 1944 to remind Americans to stay healthy during World War II. The American League Golden Anniversary patch was placed on every AL jersey in 1951 to celebrate the league's fiftieth year. Jerseys with original patches are rare and valuable.

CHAPTER 4

BASEBALL CARDS

BEFORE THE WORLD'S MOST AVID baseball collectors turned to jerseys, bats, gloves, and balls, many of them bought baseball cards. Some of them still do. They got into card collecting for the same reason everyone does: because the only thing better than baseball was the thrill of tearing open a fresh pack of cards. Little did they know that one day their baseball-card collections could be very valuable.

One leading memorabilia collector who started with baseball cards is Marshall Fogel. Mr. Fogel bought his

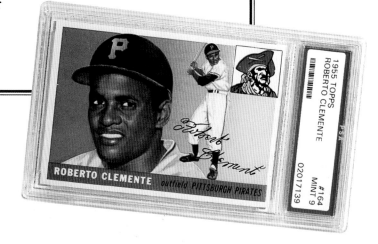

(facing page): Assortment of early 1950s baseball cards

(right): Roberto Clemente's 1955 Topps rookie card

first pack in 1953, when he was nine years old. Topps, a leading baseball-card company, had just introduced its first major card set the year before.

The father of one of Mr. Fogel's friends owned a drugstore, so Marshall and his friend got the first crack at the packs the store received. As they stuffed their faces with bubble gum, the boys shuffled through the cards. After the third card of the third pack, Marshall suddenly stopped shuffling. He had none other than the 1952 Mickey Mantle card. For a huge Yankees fan like Marshall, it was a dream come true!

"I used to put myself to sleep every night dreaming about being the Mick, Yogi, or Scooter," Mr. Fogel says of his boyhood heroes.

Today he owns many vintage baseball cards in mint condition. A card of Pee Wee Reese, issued by Bowman Gum, Inc., in 1953 (right), shows the superb Brooklyn Dodgers shortstop leaping high to turn a double play. It is the first baseball card ever to show a player in action. But one of Mr. Fogel's favorite cards of all is his 1952 Topps Mickey Mantle card. It's just like the one he had as a boy.

The most expensive baseball card on record once belonged to a collector named Brian Seigel. It is worth more than a million dollars! The card is of legendary Pittsburgh Pirates shortstop Honus Wagner. Almost a hundred years old, the card is in near-mint to

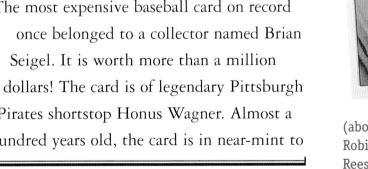

(above, top to bottom): 1956 Topps Jackie Robinson card, a 1953 Bowman Pee Wee Reese card, and the famous T206 Honus Wagner card

(left): 1952 Topps Mickey Mantle card and autographed game-used bat from the 1961 season

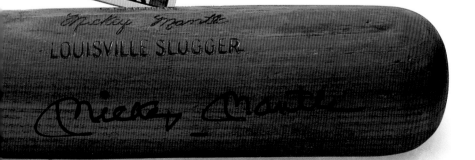

mint condition. Mr. Seigel bought it for $1.265 million in 2000 and sold it in 2007 for $2.35 million.

The Honus Wagner card is part of a set of 523 cards issued by the American Tobacco Company between 1909 and 1911. The landmark cards are known today as the T206 set. Each one features a color print of a ballplayer.

The Honus Wagner card was one of the featured cards in the 1909 set. Wagner was the star shortstop of the Pirates from 1900 to 1917. Some baseball historians say he was the best player of his era, better even than the immortal Ty Cobb. Wagner was one of the first players elected to the Hall of Fame. In the world of serious card collecting, the Wagner card is in a league of its own. It is the one card that every diehard would love to have.

This specific T206 Honus Wagner is rated 8 out of a possible 10 by a leading third-party sports-card grading service called Professional Sports Authenticator. A score of 10 means the card is in gem mint, or perfect, condition. This Wagner card is the highest-graded example known to exist. The next highest one is only a 4.

What would cause someone to spend more than a million dollars on a baseball card? Mr. Seigel collects T206 Hall of Fame cards. And the crown jewel of his T206 collection was the ultrarare Honus Wagner card. He just had to have it! Mr. Seigel now has seventy-four of the seventy-six Hall of Fame ballplayers in the

(left): Three T206 Cy Young cards

(below): Walter Johnson and Ty Cobb cards from the T206 set

MONTY IRVIN
Morford Monte Irvin

GIL McDOUGALD
Gil McDougald

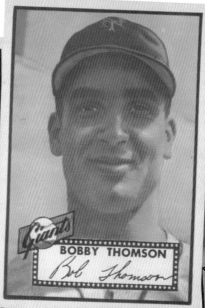

BOBBY THOMSON
Bob Thomson

DUKE SNIDER
Edwin D Snider

M. BROWN, CHICAGO NAT'L

MATHEWSON, N. Y. NAT'L

set. Amazingly, all of these cards have been graded 8 or higher by Professional Sports Authenticator.

Like Mr. Fogel, a collector named Charles Merkel bought his first baseball cards as a boy. He was ten years old when he became a lifetime New York Yankees fan and collector of baseball cards in the summer of 1952. There were no major-league teams within a thousand miles of the small town of Leland, Mississippi, where he grew up, so for vacation that summer his parents took him to St Louis. There, they caught a doubleheader between the St. Louis Browns and the Yankees. Mr. Merkel spent hours getting autographs from players. Mr. Merkel's parents snapped pictures of their son standing with Yankees stars like Mickey Mantle and Yogi Berra.

By the end of the series, just about all the Yankees had signed a ball for the kid from Mississippi. But Mr. Merkel still needed a

(facing page, top): 1952 Topps cards of Monte Irvin, Gil McDougald, Bobby Thomson, and Duke Snider

(facing page, bottom): T206 cards of pitchers Mordecai "Three Finger" Brown and Christy Mathewson

(above): 1952 Topps cards of Robin Roberts, Bob Feller, Larry Doby, who was the first African-American to play in the American League, and Willie Mays

(below): Mickey Mantle and ten-year-old Charles Merkel in the summer of 1952

signature from a rookie named Andy Carey. After the game, Yankees third baseman Gil McDougald invited him into the clubhouse to find Carey. When the players realized they were staying at the same hotel as the Merkels, they invited Charles to ride back to the hotel on the team bus!

"And the bus ride back to the hotel was probably one of the greatest thrills of my life," Mr. Merkel says. "From then on, I was hooked on the Yankees. And baseball cards became an obsession for me. I just couldn't wait to get my hands on those cards that pictured all my heroes who sat with me on the bus."

COLLECTING VINTAGE BASEBALL CARDS (1915–1970)

BIG LEAGUE CHEWING GUM

— No. 144 —
GEORGE HERMAN (BABE) RUTH
NEW YORK YANKEES

Cost Red Sox less than $3,000 in 1914, but New York Yankees paid about $125,000 for him six years later. Stepped from industrial school in Baltimore to minor league ball and went to big league in less than a year.
Was star pitcher for several years, but now plays in outfield. Holds big league home run record, 60, made in 1927. Led American League in batting in 1924. Last year batted .341 and hit 41 homers. Is 39 years old, six feet, two inches tall and weighs 210. Bats and throws left handed.

This is one of a series of 240 Baseball Stars
BIG LEAGUE
CHEWING GUM
GOUDEY GUM CO.   BOSTON
Made by the originators of
INDIAN GUM

JOE DI MAGGIO, Yankees

"TED" WILLIAMS

One of the great things about baseball-card collecting is that it never gets old. Every season there are new cards to collect.

Vintage cards can be divided into two major categories: those that were printed before World War II (1941–1945) and those that came after. A popular prewar set, the first to ever include bubble gum, was issued by the Goudey Gum Company of Boston in 1933. The Goudey set featured nearly every star of the day, including multiple cards of "big name" players like Dizzy Dean, Lefty Grove, and Carl Hubbell.

NAPOLEON   (LARRY) LAJOIE

Each pack came with a note saying there were 240 cards in the series. In fact, there were only 239. Card 106 was missing from every set! Goudey Gum Company had sent collectors in the United States on a wild goose chase. It worked: Packs sold out everywhere as kids tried to find the missing card. Goudey finally issued 106 the following year, in 1934. It pictured Dead Ball era legend Napoleon Lajoie, who had been retired for eighteen years. The card is now one of the scarcest and most valuable on the market.

Another important set was issued by Gum, Inc., between 1939 and 1941. It is known as the Play Ball series. In 1941 the company issued just 72 cards. All of them are in full color and the set is considered one of the most beautiful ever produced. Today's collectors cherish the 1941 Play Ball set.

During World War II, paper shortages ended baseball-card collecting for several years. The first major set after the war was issued in 1948 by Bowman Gum Inc., the direct descendant of the company that made the Play Ball set.

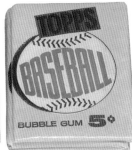

Another pioneering baseball card company was Topps. The company issued its first set of cards in 1951, and the cards didn't even come with bubble gum. The next year, Topps created full-color "giant" cards that were 50 percent larger than the cards issued by Bowman that same year. Collectors bought them up as fast as they could. Experts say the Topps 1952 series is the most impressive and important of all postwar card issues. The set's Mickey Mantle card is now the most sought-after postwar card of all.

A vintage card's value is determined by many different things, including rarity, condition, and popularity. A rare card of a popular player in great condition is the most valuable. The majority of sports-cards grading services, like Professional Sports Authenticator, rate cards on a scale of 1 to 10. Two identical cards can be worth different amounts if one is in better shape than the other.

For most collectors, cards are really about fun, not money.

(facing page, top): 1951 Bowman Mickey Mantle card; both the front and back of the 1933 Goudey Gum Babe Ruth card; 1938 Goudey Gum "Heads-Up" Joe DiMaggio card; 1941 Ted Williams card from the Play Ball series; (bottom): 1933 Goudey Gum card of Napoleon Lajoie that was actually issued in 1934 because it was the missing card #106 from the 1933 set

(above left): Box of 1960 Topps 5-cent unopened wax packs

(above right): 1952 Bowman card of Stan "the Man" Musial; 1953 Bowman card of Yogi Berra, part of the first baseball card set to ever feature actual color photographs

(below): 1949 Bowman Satchel Paige card; 1950 Bowman Jackie Robinson card; 1948 Leaf Babe Ruth card, issued the year the Bambino died

LEROY "Satchell" PAIGE

BABE RUTH

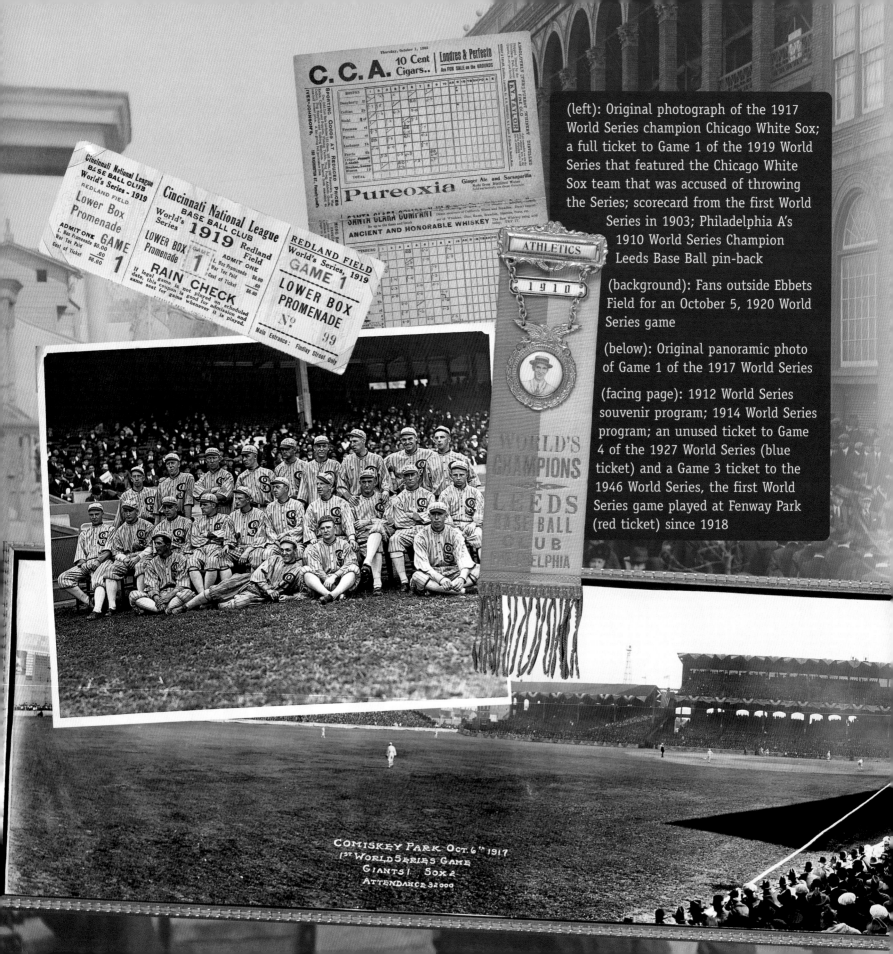

(left): Original photograph of the 1917 World Series champion Chicago White Sox; a full ticket to Game 1 of the 1919 World Series that featured the Chicago White Sox team that was accused of throwing the Series; scorecard from the first World Series in 1903; Philadelphia A's 1910 World Series Champion Leeds Base Ball pin-back

(background): Fans outside Ebbets Field for an October 5, 1920 World Series game

(below): Original panoramic photo of Game 1 of the 1917 World Series

(facing page): 1912 World Series souvenir program; 1914 World Series program; an unused ticket to Game 4 of the 1927 World Series (blue ticket) and a Game 3 ticket to the 1946 World Series, the first World Series game played at Fenway Park (red ticket) since 1918

THE WORLD SERIES

FOR PURE EXCITEMENT, nothing comes close to the World Series. In the annual showdown between National League and American League pennant winners, legends are born and dynasties are made. Year after year, the Fall Classic, as the Series is nicknamed, dishes out baseball's ultimate thrills and chills. The combination of history and excitement has helped create a booming market for World Series memorabilia.

How about Game 3 of the 1932 Series? That's when mighty Babe Ruth of the New York Yankees stood at the

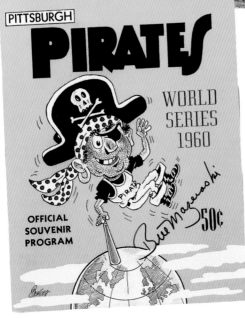

(top): Panoramic photograph of the inaugural Negro League World Series in 1924

(above): 1960 World Series program signed by Bill Mazeroski, who ended the Series with a ninth-inning blast

(facing page): Front of a scorecard from the first World Series in 1903 and a 1942 World Series program that reflects the country's patriotic wartime spirit

plate and allegedly pointed to the center-field bleachers of Chicago's Wrigley Field. The Babe then slugged the very next pitch into that exact spot. The feat became famous as Ruth's "called-shot" home run.

Another unforgettable moment came in Game 7 of the 1960 World Series between the underdog Pittsburgh Pirates and the fearsome Yankees. With the score tied at 9-9 in the bottom of the ninth, Pittsburgh second baseman Bill Mazeroski stepped up to the plate. Most hometown fans expected the game to go into extra innings. Mazeroski surprised everyone, though, by belting a home run off Yankee reliever Ralph Terry. It was the first time anyone had ever hit a homer to end a World Series.

With all that history and excitement, it's no wonder the Fall Classic appeals to baseball collectors. One of the best collections commemorating the World Series belongs to James David Clister and his daughter Lauren Alexandra, two fans from Pittsburgh. This father-daughter team collects World Series scorecards and programs. Some items in their collection go back to the earliest years of the World Series, which was first played in 1903.

The colorful items in the Clisters' collection were first sold to fans at the ballparks of each team playing in the World Series. In the early days, teams celebrated the World Series by printing scorecards on heavy paper. The covers usually showed pictures of home-team players and managers. Inside were charts that could be used to keep track of each team's batting results, inning by inning.

Scorecards for spectators at games first caught on around 1870. They were pretty plain, with black-and-white pictures and simple grids for keeping score. With the birth of the World Series, scorecards became even fancier, with larger photographs, better designs, and lots of advertisements.

Before long, teams started creating special programs for the World Series. As well as the usual scoring grids, the larger souvenir programs included biographies of players, cartoon drawings, and images of ballparks, managers, players, team mascots, and team logos. World Series programs quickly became the favorite souvenirs of fans.

SOUVENIR CARD 10 CENTS

McGREEVY
On the Avenue
Nuff said . . . .
3rd Base

1903

.. SOUVENIR CARD ..

OF THE

World's Championship Games

Boston vs. Pittsburg

OFFICIAL PROGRAM • TWENTY-FIVE CENTS

1942 WORLD SERIES

Buy
WAR BONDS
AND
STAMPS
★

NEW YORK YANKEES ★ ST. LOUIS CARDINALS

Some of the scorecards and programs in the Clisters' World Series collection have been neatly dated, marked, and in some cases scored by the lucky fans who first held them. A number of them come from some of the most exciting games in Fall Classic history. The Clisters own marked scorecards from Game 3 of the 1905 Series, Game 2 of the 1911 Series, and Game 6 of the 1947 Series.

Another scorecard in the collection marks one of the greatest individual performances in World Series history. In Game 1 of the 1967 Series between the St. Louis Cardinals and the Boston Red Sox, Cardinals outfielder and future Hall of Famer Lou Brock notched four hits, stole two bases, and scored both St. Louis runs in a 2-1 victory. Brock and the Cardinals went on to win the Series four games to three.

The Clisters' treasured World Series mementos are like stepping stones back in time. They help connect today's players, teams, and fans to the excitement of Octobers long past, when stars of yesteryear put their marks on the rich history of the World Series.

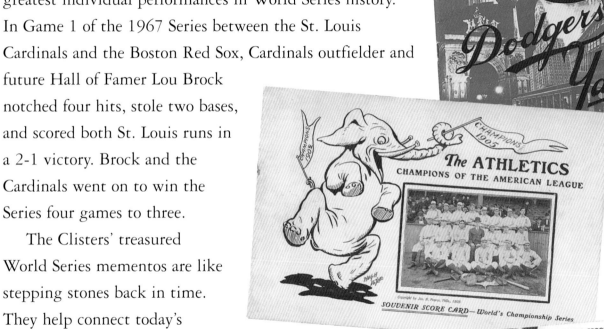

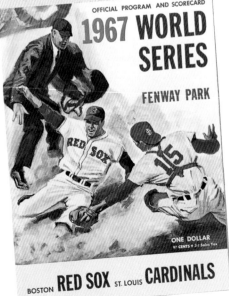

WORLD SERIES 1963

YANKEE STADIUM · HOME OF CHAMPIONS · OFFICIAL PROGRAM 50 CENTS

NEW YORK **YANKEES** LOS ANGELES **DODGERS**

(facing page, from top): 1947 World Series program reflects the all–New York series; 1905 World Series scorecard; 1967 World Series program

(above): 1963 World Series program

(above right, from top): 1926 World Series official scorecard; 1932 World Series program

(right): 1911 World Series program produced by the Philadelphia A's—a rematch of the 1905 Series

(far right): 1911 World Series program produced by the New York Giants

Montage of artifacts from the Brooklyn Dodgers, who won their only World Series in 1955

CHAPTER 6

TROPHIES

BASEBALL PLAYERS TALK ABOUT IT all the time. They want to "win a ring." That means going to the World Series and taking home the championship. The tradition of awarding special rings to World Series and pennant champs goes back a hundred years. The prize in the early days was a golden medallion a player could wear on his pocket watch. Today, it's a ring encrusted with jewels. The idea is the same: when a team proves it's the best, the team owner rewards players and coaches with special gifts to commemorate the season.

(above): Trophy cup given by J. L. Wilkinson, owner of the Negro National League's Kansas City Monarchs, to José Mendez for leading the Monarchs to victory in the 1924 inaugural Negro League World Series

(above right) Willie Mays, Don Mueller, and Dusty Rhodes show off their 1954 New York Giants World Series rings.

(right): 1. 1949 New York Yankees World Series ring; 2. 1955 Brooklyn Dodgers World Series ring; 3. 1993 Toronto Blue Jays World Series ring

Roy Campanella's 1955 National League MVP Award, the third of his career; Campanella accepts his 1955 MVP Award.

Just as some collectors specialize in cards or jerseys, others passionately pursue championship rings, World Series trophies, and other official baseball awards. At the highest level of collecting, the list of top trophies to have includes Most Valuable Player Awards, given every year to the single best player in each league; Gold Glove Awards, awarded to the best fielders at each position; and Batting Crowns, won by the player with the highest season batting average in each league.

A baseball fan named Ron Leff and his two sons, Andy and Mitchell, have built a major-league collection of baseball trophies. The fantastic Leff Family Collection includes trophies won by some of baseball's greatest players and teams, including American and National League MVP Awards, World Series trophies, and a glittering assortment of championship rings.

The modern MVP Award was born in 1930. That year, the Baseball Writers' Association of America (BBWAA) formed a committee of sportswriters to select an MVP for each league. The BBWAA Most Valuable Player Award is still baseball's top individual prize. Along with bragging rights, MVP winners receive the Kenesaw Mountain Landis Memorial Baseball Award trophy, a plaque named for Major League Baseball's first commissioner.

Ron Leff and his sons own two Landis trophies. They got the plate-shaped gold and silver trophies directly from the families of winning players. One was awarded to Brooklyn

Mickey Mantle's 1962 American League MVP Award, the third of his career

[46]

Dodgers catcher Roy Campanella in 1955. The Dodgers won their one and only World Series that year. The Leffs' other trophy once belonged to Yankees Hall of Famer Mickey Mantle. He won it for the 1962 season, when he helped the Yanks win their seventh World Series title since his rookie season in 1951. Campanella and Mantle each won three MVP Awards.

In 1949, the Hillerich & Bradsby Company, makers of the famous Louisville Slugger bat, began giving the Silver Bat Award to the player in each league with the highest season batting average. Weighing in at 56 ounces and measuring 34 inches in length, Silver Bats were engraved with the H & B company logo, the player's name, and his batting average.

The Leff Family Collection includes the Silver Bat awarded to Willie Mays in 1954, probably the best season the terrific Mays ever had. He had the highest batting average in the National League (.345), won the league MVP, and led his New York Giants to a World Series sweep over the Cleveland Indians.

In 1957, Rawlings Sporting Goods of St. Louis established the Gold Glove Award to recognize excellence in fielding. The selection process changed twice before 1965, and now managers and coaches from each team select the winners.

Some of baseball's most unique trophies commemorate World Series victories and player milestones. The massive gold-plated World Series trophy features pennants inscribed with the name of every major league team. The flags

(above): Willie Mays's 1954 Silver Bat, awarded for having the highest batting average (.345) in the National League for that season

(below): Mickey Mantle (middle, with Ralph Terry, left, and Tom Tresh, right) holds his MVP trophy from 1962, when he hit .321 with 30 home runs and 89 RBIs.

surround a silver baseball engraved with the year. A golden crown sits on top of a gold band above the ball, and a pair of World Series press pins representing the two Series teams rests in front. Sometimes, winning teams give an outstanding player a personal model of the huge Series trophy. The Yankees honored terrific center fielder Mickey Rivers with a replica in 1978. The Toronto Blue Jays did the same thing for second baseman Roberto Alomar in 1992.

After Ernie Banks hit his 500th career home run for the Cubs in 1970, National League president Charles "Chub" Feeney presented him with a special trophy that now is in the Leff collection. The trophy lists every single one of Banks's 500 home runs. From top to bottom, it stands nearly four feet tall. It is one of only a few 500-home-run trophies given to players in that exclusive club known to exist in a private collection.

Another one-of-a-kind trophy owned by the Leffs was created for New York Yankees pitcher Don Larsen in 1956. That year, Larsen pitched a perfect game in Game 5 of the World Series. Twenty-seven Brooklyn Dodgers went up to the plate, and not one of them made it to first base. It was the first perfect game in World Series history. No pitcher has ever done it again.

"Sometimes a week might go by when I don't think of that game," Larsen once said. "But I don't remember when it happened last." The trophy is a sterling reminder of the many amazing achievements—and surprises—that make baseball America's game.

(facing page, top): 1992 World Series Champions trophy presented to Roberto Alomar by the Toronto Blue Jays for his MVP performance in the Series; Ernie Banks was awarded this special trophy by Major League Baseball to commemorate his 500th home run; the flyer handed out during Banks's Hall of Fame induction; (bottom): Steve Carlton's 1981 Gold Glove Award; Philadelphia Phillies third baseman Mike Schmidt's first Gold Glove Award from 1976—he would win 10 total; Tony Gwynn's 1991 Gold Glove Award— his last of five won during his career with the San Diego Padres

(above): Yogi Berra leaps into Don Larsen's arms after Larsen threw the only perfect game in World Series history.

(left): A bronzed commemorative trophy of Larsen's perfect game includes his glove, spikes, hat, and the ball caught by Berra for the final out.

CHAPTER 7

FOR THE LOVE OF BASEBALL

GROWING UP NEAR SAN FRANCISCO, in Los Altos Hills, California, I loved baseball. I played second base with a brief stint as pitcher in the Los Altos Little League. My favorite major-league team naturally was the San Francisco Giants, and my favorite player was Willie Mays; who else? He was the greatest Giant who ever lived. I just wish I had been old enough to see this legend play!

I spent many windy afternoons and evenings watching Giants games at Candlestick Park, the coldest ballpark on earth! I remember very clearly my first trip to Candlestick.

(facing page): A montage of artifacts from two legendary rivals who defined baseball during the 1940s: Ted Williams and Joe DiMaggio

(above): A tribute to the Say Hey Kid: Willie Mays's hat from the 1954 season, his game-used glove from the 1957 season, his unaltered game-worn jersey from the 1959 season, and a full ticket from Game 1 of the 1954 World Series when Mays made "the Catch"

(right): Stephen Wong gets ready for his 1975 Little League game.

(above): Original news service photo shows the heart of the Boys of Summer (Duke Snider, Gil Hodges, Jackie Robinson, Pee Wee Reese, and Roy Campanella) at Ebbets Field on June 6, 1951; 1954 Topps Henry Aaron rookie card

(facing page): 1909 game-worn jerseys of the famous Chicago Cubs double-play trio Joe Tinker, Johnny Evers, and Frank Chance, along with season passes from the 1909 and 1910 seasons and their T205 cards

It was the summer of 1975. I was eight. I remember crystal blue skies, the smell of hot dogs and roasted peanuts, and a brisk wind coming off the bay. Already a budding collector, I brought a stack of my 1975 Topps baseball cards to the game.

The first vintage baseball card I ever owned was a 1965 Topps baseball card of Hank Aaron. I bought it for three dollars from a store called the Dugout in Mountain View, California, about a thirty-minute bicycle ride from my house. Riding back home with the card safely tucked away, I was nearly giddy with joy. I could hardly believe it was really mine.

I continued to collect baseball cards after I went off to high school at the Lawrenceville School in New Jersey. In my sophomore year, I discovered something that made baseball even more important to me. While researching a paper, I wandered into the basement of the school library to find some books. There I came upon some of the school's old yearbooks dating back to the late 1800s. I found a newspaper clipping stuck between two pages of a yearbook from around 1910 containing the poem "Baseball's Sad Lexicon" by American columnist Franklin Pierce Adams:

These are the saddest of possible words:
"Tinker to Evers to Chance."
Trio of Bear Cubs and Fleeter than birds,
"Tinker to Evers to Chance."
Ruthlessly pricking our gonfalon bubble,
Making a Giant hit into a double,
Words that are weighty with nothing but trouble:
"Tinker to Evers to Chance."

(above): Original 1929 autographed photo of (left to right) the Chicago Cubs' Rogers Hornsby, Hack Wilson, Charlie Grimm, Kiki Cuyler, and Riggs Stephenson

(facing page, top): Dizzy Dean's jersey from the 1934 season when he won the National League MVP, along with his brother Daffy Dean's jersey from 1936. In 1934, the two brothers combined to win four games of the World Series as the St. Louis Cardinals defeated the Detroit Tigers. The tickets from all seven games of that Series are visible.

(facing page, bottom): Original photograph of the 1906 Chicago White Sox, who were nicknamed the "Hitless Wonders" since they were able to win the World Series despite having a team batting average of .230, the lowest ever for a championship team

I had no idea who Tinker, Evers, and Chance were. I didn't know what "gonfalon bubble" meant. And the poem certainly had nothing to do with the paper I was supposed to be writing. But I was curious. Who were Tinker and Evers and Chance? Why were they the subjects of a poem? I had to know.

To find out, I began reading every book I could find on early baseball. I became fascinated by the sport's rich history and by early twentieth-century ballplayers. Many of the players were the children and grandchildren of immigrants. I could relate to that. My parents were originally from Hong Kong.

From my reading, I learned that Joe Tinker, Johnny Evers, and Frank Chance were the shortstop, the second baseman, and the first baseman, respectively, for the Chicago Cubs in the early twentieth century. They were famous for turning one double play after another. A gonfalon, it turned out, was a royal flag. By completing double plays against the Giants, Tinker, Evers, and Chance spoiled the Giants' dream of winning another kind of flag: the National League pennant. They burst the bubble of Giants fans.

The more I read, the more interested I became. I started collecting old baseball cards so that I could see the faces of the players I was reading so much about. Soon, I was buying old scorecards as well as baseball cards. Collecting made me feel closer to the history of the game and all the great players of the past. Prices then were really low compared with today's, so even though I was still a student I was able to afford many items. Before long, I decided to focus my collection on the special bonds between certain players—such as Tinker, Evers, and Chance, forever linked by their clocklike teamwork in turning double plays.

In baseball, there are many kinds of bonds. There are blood bonds between brothers (pitchers Dizzy and Daffy Dean), bonds of greatness (rivals Ted Williams and Joe DiMaggio), bonds of friendship (1940s and 1950s Red Sox teammates Ted Williams, Bobby Doerr, Johnny Pesky, and Dominic DiMaggio—Joe's brother!), and social bonds (the Brooklyn Dodgers of the late 1940s and 1950s, baseball's first racially integrated team). All have a special place in my collection.

The Wong Family Archives Collection pays tribute to these friends, teammates, brothers, and mutually respectful rivals. It honors their achievements as baseball players and also as friends and peers. They were men who shared many experiences together not only on the diamond and in dugouts and locker rooms but also on trolleys, trains, and buses, and at diners, hotels, and one another's homes. My collection honors the emotions they felt for one another, and the memories they gave to fans.

I think the best way for young collectors to get started today is to do what I did. Read high-quality baseball books and learn about the game's rich heritage. Collectors should also try to attend baseball memorabilia conventions. The king of them all is the National Sports Collectors Convention. The key guiding principle is to collect what you like.

(right): Original photograph from May 2, 1939, the day Lou "the Iron Horse" Gehrig pulled himself from the Yankees lineup, ending a streak of 2,130 consecutive games played

(below right): 1952 Topps Mickey Mantle card

(below): Circa-1910 advertisement for Colgan's Chips chewing gum features the likeness of Pittsburgh shortstop Honus Wagner.

My favorite piece of memorabilia as a kid was, hands down, the 1952 Topps Mickey Mantle card. Today, I have two favorites. The first is Lou Gehrig's New York Yankees road-style game-worn jersey that he wore during the 1937, 1938, and 1939 seasons. The second is an original photograph by Cleveland's first newspaper staff photographer, Louis Van Oeyen (1865–1946), of the All-Star team that played in the July 24, 1911 Addie Joss Day Benefit Game. One item I would really like to add to my collection is a baseball painting called *Saturday Afternoon at Sportsman's Park*. The artist Edward Lanning made the painting in 1944, when Sportsman's was home to the St. Louis Cardinals, the team of brothers Dizzy and Daffy Dean. Sportsman's Park was torn down in 1966. The ball field that replaced it, Busch Stadium, was itself recently replaced by a new one in St. Louis. That kind of history, the way players and teams and ballparks connect us to a bygone era, is one reason I will always be a collector.

We are very blessed to have the game of baseball, a sport that has inspired so many generations of fans, writers, poets, musicians, and movie producers of all backgrounds. Woven into the fabric of baseball's history are traits that deeply reflect the very soul of America, both good and bad: the spirit of invention and ingenuity, heroism, sacrifice, greed, bigotry, compassion, greatness, and failure. To me, baseball represents a constant reminder of a time from which so many of our collective blessings flow. The history of the game and its vibrant traditions can bring comfort and build continuity, connecting us with the past. Baseball allows us all to hold on to a piece of our childhood. And that's very special.

(below): Original July 24, 1911 photograph of the American League All-Star team that played against the Cleveland Naps in the Addie Joss Day Benefit Game

(bottom): Sportsman's Park in St. Louis